My Little Golden Book About Country Music

By Maisy Carter

Illustrated by Monique Dong

A GOLDEN BOOK • NEW YORK

Golden Books
An imprint of Random House Children's Books
A division of Penguin Random House LLC
1745 Broadway, New York, NY 10019
penguinrandomhouse.com
rhcbooks.com

Library of Congress Control Number: 2025934105
ISBN 979-8-217-11656-0 (trade) — ISBN 979-8-217-11657-7 (ebook)
Manufactured in the United States of America
10 9 8 7 6 5 4 3 2 1
EU Contact: Penguin Random House Ireland, 32 Nassau Street, Dublin D02 YH68.
https://eu-contact.penguin.ie

Country music is in big cities and small towns. It's enjoyed across America and around the world. But it all started in the southern Appalachian Mountains in the early 1900s, when people combined gospel, blues, and folk music to make new sounds. In 1927, a talent scout went to Bristol, Tennessee, to record some of those songs and country music was born!

Some of the earliest country-music stars were recorded at the Bristol Sessions.

The Carter Family—A. P. Carter; his wife, Sara Carter; and Sara's cousin Maybelle Carter—played guitar and sang harmonies. They recorded more than three hundred songs during their long career.

Jimmie Rodgers was nicknamed the Singing Brakeman because he worked on railroads before becoming a musician. He was famous for a kind of singing called yodeling. His song "Blue Yodel" was one of the first big hits in country music.

Country music spread to Hollywood in the 1930s and '40s. Western movies featuring actors like Gene Autry and Roy Rogers—known as singing cowboys—made country music even more popular.

You didn't have to go to the movie theater to hear country songs. People from all over the US tuned in to the *Grand Ole Opry,* a live radio show from Nashville, Tennessee. All the big stars performed at the Opry—and they still do today!

Bill Monroe debuted on the show in 1939 with his band the Blue Grass Boys. The high-pitched singing and fast strumming on instruments, including Bill's mandolin, led to a new type of country music called bluegrass.

Hank Williams first performed at the Opry in 1949.
The audience liked him so much, he received six encores!
He became one of the biggest country stars of all time
thanks to songs like "Lovesick Blues" and "Hey, Good
Lookin'." He helped make honky-tonk—a style of
country music that was good for dancing—popular.

Charley Pride is considered the first Black country-music star. He grew up listening to the *Grand Ole Opry,* and in 1967, he was the first Black solo singer to perform on the radio show. He sang two songs that night, including one by Hank Williams. Over the course of his country career, Charley had twenty-nine number one hits!

Before becoming a famous musician, he was also making hits—with a bat instead of a guitar! Charley was a professional baseball player in both the Negro American League and the minor league.

Country music usually includes stringed instruments like guitar and mandolin. Here are some other instruments you might hear:

Most country songs tell stories about people's lives.
Some are happy stories. Some are sad stories. But they're
all stories that listeners can connect to.

Loretta Lynn's song "Coal Miner's Daughter" tells the
story of her childhood growing up poor in Kentucky.

George Jones's "He Stopped Loving Her Today" is
a love story and considered one of the greatest songs in
country music.

Kenny Rogers shared some
advice for playing cards in his
catchy song "The Gambler."

Dolly Parton is one of the biggest country stars of all time. She wrote her first song when she was just five years old and went on to write thousands more! The song closest to her heart is "Coat of Many Colors," a true story from her childhood. She has written songs made popular by other singers like Waylon Jennings, Emmylou Harris, and Whitney Houston.

Dolly is also famous for her generosity. She founded Dolly Parton's Imagination Library, which sends millions of free books to children around the world.

Country musicians also have a real flair for fashion!
In the early days, performers often wore gingham, plaid,
and overalls. Many of today's stars still wear clothes
inspired by cowboys and the West—like cowboy hats and
boots, jeans, and belts with shiny buckles.

Some dress up in sparkly rhinestone suits and sequined gowns. Others keep it casual in T-shirts and baseball caps.

Patsy Cline often wore cowgirl outfits with lots of fringe. One of her most famous songs, "Crazy," came out in 1961 and was a hit on the country *and* pop charts.

Johnny Cash was famous for his deep voice and for wearing all black when he was onstage. He sang a kind of country called outlaw music.

Shania Twain is known as the Queen of Country Pop thanks to hit songs like "You're Still the One." She has a unique style all her own—and a love of leopard print.

You can recognize Willie Nelson by his long braids and bandana. His song "On the Road Again" is one of the most loved in country music. And he was the songwriter behind Patsy Cline's hit "Crazy."

The King of Country, George Strait, is known for selling more than sixty million records since 1981 and for his classic cowboy look—from the hat straight down to the boots.

Garth Brooks is also known for wearing cowboy hats—and for being the best-selling country musician of all time!

Lainey Wilson wears bell-bottoms, pants that get wider from the knees to the hems, just about every day. She named her 2022 album *Bell Bottom Country*. And in 2023, she won five Country Music Association Awards, including Entertainer of the Year—while wearing extra-fancy bell-bottoms, of course.

Country-music artists are hardworking performers who found fame in different ways.

The First Lady of Country Music, Tammy Wynette, worked as a hairdresser before she made it big. Her 1968 song "Stand by Your Man" is one of the top-selling singles in country-music history!

Reba McEntire was discovered at the age of nineteen when she sang the national anthem at a rodeo. She went on to be named the Country Music Association's Best Female Vocalist four years in a row!

Did you know Taylor Swift started her career in country music? Her family moved to Nashville when she was thirteen years old so she could follow her dream of being a country-music star.

Carrie Underwood won the television show *American Idol* in 2005. She's been winning awards and selling out concert arenas ever since!

Kane Brown got his start taking videos of himself singing and posting them on social media. In 2017, he became the first artist ever to reach the top of all five of the *Billboard* country-music charts!

Kacey Musgraves was a competitive yodeler as a kid and voted Most Likely to Become Famous by her high school class. In 2018, she won Album of the Year at the Grammys, the Academy of Country Music Awards, *and* the Country Music Association Awards!

Beyoncé was already a hip-hop and pop-music legend when she tried something new with her album *Cowboy Carter*. In 2025, she became the first Black artist to win Best Country Album at the Grammys!

Nashville is considered the country music capital of the world. If you visit the city, you can eat at the Bluebird Café where Taylor Swift, Faith Hill, Garth Brooks, and Trisha Yearwood have all performed. You can see the Grand Ole Opry, where artists, including Miranda Lambert, Tim McGraw, Blake Shelton, Keith Urban, Darius Rucker, and Luke Combs, have sung their biggest hits.

And you can find out more about country stars from the past and present at the Country Music Hall of Fame and Museum.

There are many, many other talented country artists who have entertained and inspired fans of all ages with their music. What are the names of your favorites?

Who knows . . . Maybe the next country star
could be you!